Birmingham Railways

IN OLD PHOTOGRAPHS

Birmingham Railways

IN OLD PHOTOGRAPHS

Collected by MIKE HITCHES

ALAN SUTTON

Alan Sutton Publishing Limited
Phoenix Mill · Far Thrupp · Stroud · Gloucestershire

First published 1992

British Library Cataloguing in Publication Data

Hitches, Mike
  Birmingham Railways in Old Photographs
  I. Title
  385.09424

  ISBN 0-7509-0027-X

DEDICATION: To Mam and Dad

Typeset in 10/11 Sabon.
Typesetting and origination by
Alan Sutton Publishing Limited.
Printed in Great Britain by
The Bath Press, Avon.

Contents

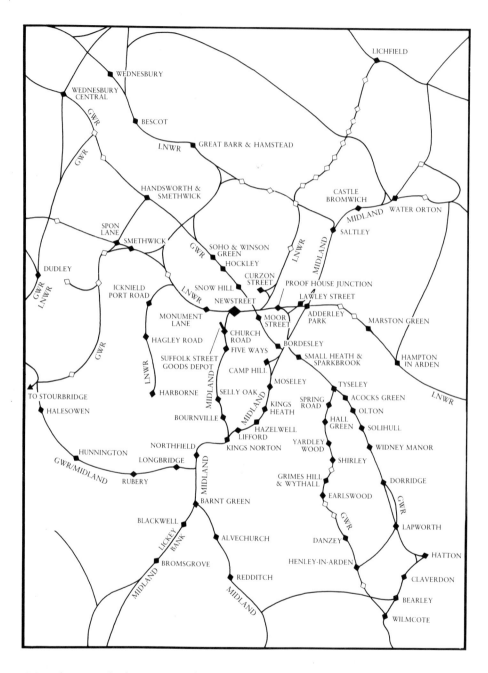

Map showing the lines covered in this book.

Introduction

Being Britain's second city and a major industrial centre, Birmingham has been well served by railways since the Grand Junction Railway, which operated a line between Liverpool and Birmingham, opened in 1837. The following year the London and Birmingham Railway was opened and the town became a major hub between the north-western seaports and the capital city. Other companies brought railways into the town as it expanded in an effort to take advantage of possible revenues from transport of raw materials and finished products for the many hundreds of industries being established there. In 1840 the Birmingham and Gloucester Railway was opened as far as Cheltenham from a temporary terminus at Camp Hill, close to Birmingham town centre. A few years later the company's trains ran through to the London and Birmingham Railway's terminus at Curzon Street, even closer to the centre. The Great Western Railway began to take an interest in this line when it amalgamated with the Gloucester and Bristol Railway and its 4 ft 8 ½ in gauge line encroached on the 7 ft gauge of the GWR. The GWR also saw an opportunity to have its own gauge invade the territory of the L&BR who were the main force behind adoption of the smaller gauge as standard for Britain's railways. Their plans were thwarted when the line from Birmingham to Bristol was bought by the Midland Railway, thus preserving 'narrow gauge' interests. To add insult to injury, this line has always been seen as the most important route from Birmingham to the West Country, despite the many attempts of the GWR to compete for this traffic on what should have been natural territory for them. The GWR did, however, establish a presence in Birmingham when they took control of the Oxford and Birmingham Railway in 1848. The line itself opened in 1852 and terminated at a modest wooden station which was to become the popular and affectionately remembered Snow Hill.

The first stations in Birmingham were Lawley Street, of the Grand Junction Railway, and Curzon Street, of the London and Birmingham Railway. Curzon Street entrance was through a Doric arch, similar to the one at Euston which was destroyed by the corporate vandalism so prevalent in the 1960s when Euston was rebuilt by British Railways. Curzon Street arch is now preserved and used as offices. It can be seen on the left, in the middle of a goods yard, from trains leaving New Street for London. Both Curzon Street and Lawley Street were some way out of the centre of Birmingham and there were fears that women would be at risk passing through dimly lit streets as they made their way from the stations to the town centre. Plans were drawn up for a station closer to the centre, and New Street was opened in 1854 after the GJR and L&BR had become part of the London and North Western Railway from 1846. The station was used jointly by the LNWR and the Midland Railway, who were given access to the new station as a 'thank you' for keeping the broad gauge of the GWR out of their territory. The Midland went on to build an extension to New Street for their own use. Curzon Street and Lawley Street were developed into large goods yards when New Street came into use.

All trains operating out of Curzon Street and Lawley Street were transferred to New Street, including trains operating along the Camp Hill line to Bristol. The Camp Hill route was, however, rather circuitous as it wound its way west. This problem was remedied when the Birmingham West Suburban Line was brought into New Street in 1885. The line was opened in 1876, from a terminus in Granville Street, as a single-line branch to Kings Norton where it formed a junction with the Camp Hill line. The Midland Railway took control of the line in 1875 and set about planning a connection with New Street. In an Act of 1881 approval was given for a line into New Street and for doubling of the BWSR track. When the extension was opened Granville Street station was closed and a new one opened at Five Ways. Once this work was complete, express traffic to Bristol was transferred to the BWSR and the Camp Hill line became a branch, but one used for traffic which needed to avoid the increasingly congested New Street.

The Midland Line from Birmingham to Bristol is famous for one of the steepest climbs in England, the Lickey Bank, which has a gradient of 1 in 37 and has been the bane of many a fireman who has struggled to maintain steam as his engine climbs. The steepness of the bank has ensured that powerful engines have been based at Bromsgrove, including one specially built for the job, solely to provide assistance for heavy trains as they climbed. Modern high-speed train sets climb the bank as though it didn't exist and fail to give any impression of the hard labour that was once required of man and machine to conquer this difficult climb.

Snow Hill station was improved in 1871, when the original station building was removed to Didcot, a more substantial structure being built following improved services to Paddington. The station was completely remodelled in 1906, and it was this station that continued to exist until closure in March 1972, only for a new station to reopen in 1989. Increasing traffic demands brought problems at Snow Hill and the GWR built a terminus station at Moor Street in 1909 to deal with suburban traffic from Leamington Spa and the new North Warwickshire Line from Stratford-upon-Avon. Moor Street also dealt with excursion trains from London and the West Country which could not be accommodated at Snow Hill. A traverser, which was large enough to carry a 'Castle' class 4-6-0, was provided to allow engines to clear the buffer stops. Moor Street closed in 1989 when a new, adjacent station was opened as part of the new Snow Hill project.

When Birmingham became a City in 1889, three railway companies, the LNWR, the GWR, and the Midland were providing train services. The GWR and Midland had services to the West Country, the LNWR and GWR had two-hour services to London (although the LNWR was always seen as the major provider of London trains), the Midland had services to Derby and the north-east of England, the LNWR ran trains to the north-west of England, North Wales, and Scotland, and the GWR ran trains to South Wales. There were also numerous commuter trains from many local stations bringing passengers into the city from the new suburbs, and numerous freight trains to supply the city's industries. Traffic demands for the city meant that all three companies had motive power depots to provide the locomotives required. The GWR had a shed at Tyseley, the Midland had depots at Saltley and Bournville, and the LNWR had facilities at Monument Lane, Aston and Bescot.

Many of the city's industries had railways within their factories, linking firms with the national system, to bring in raw materials and take out finished goods. Sadly, virtually all of these railways have now gone as road traffic provides the necessary transport infrastructure, although, ironically, the Rover Group at Longbridge does still use the railway to transport many of the cars manufactured at its works.

Despite the industrial nature of Birmingham, many of the lines radiating from the city centre appear to run through seemingly rural landscapes, while others give an idea of the importance of industry to the city's development. Some lines, notably the ex-LNWR line to Wolverhampton and the ex-Midland line to Bristol, run parallel with that other great transport innovation predating the railways, the canals.

This book recalls the heyday of Birmingham's railways from the late nineteenth century to the mid-1950s, when British Railways' 'Modernisation Plan' was introduced, which would see mass withdrawals of steam locomotives over the following decade. Much of the main-line railway infrastructure remains today, even after Dr Beeching introduced his infamous report recommending many closures in the city. The North Warwickshire Line was to close, but lives on thanks to the efforts of the Action Committee, and the line is very well used but still has to fight for survival. The West Suburban Line had its commuter services run down, but now has an important role in rapid transit within the city as part of the 'Cross-City' service between Redditch and Lichfield via New Street, and is currently being electrified. Some lines did close, however, although with road traffic congestion in the city being what it is, there is potential for many reopenings.

I hope these photographs will bring back memories of the myriad railway services that operated within the city and its surrounding areas. An expatriate 'Brummie' myself, sorting through the photographs of my home town railways has recalled youthful days train-spotting in many of these locations.

The London and North Western Railway

As far as Birmingham was concerned, the LNWR was the 'Premier Line' in more ways than one. Two of the companies that were amalgamated to form the LNWR in 1846 were the first to bring railways into the city: the Grand Junction Railway, which opened its route between Manchester and Birmingham in 1837, closely followed by the London and Birmingham Railway, whose line opened in 1838.

The L&BR line was always the most important route to London, and remained so despite the efforts of the GWR to attract passengers to their services. A trip to London usually meant travelling from New Street to Euston rather than from Snow Hill to Paddington. Even today, the majority of trains for London use the original L&BR line to Euston.

The LNWR became part of the London, Midland and Scottish Railway at the 'Grouping' in 1923, along with the Midland Railway, and ran trains from New Street to the north-west of England using the old GJR route, and to North Wales via the major junction at Crewe. The north-west was an important business route, and the North Wales coast became popular with 'Brummies' for seaside holidays and excursion trips.

There were also local services to the north-west of the city and the Black Country, and along the London route to Coventry. These lines also carried freight to supply the many industries of Birmingham with raw materials, coal and steel from the north-west and Black Country, and slate from North Wales quarries for building an expanding Birmingham.

New Street is now the only station for express services from Birmingham, the centre for trains to most destinations in Britain, and, despite complete rebuilding as part of the electrification scheme of the 1960s and subsequent loss of character, remains a tribute to the LNWR.

Birmingham's first major station was at Curzon Street, and opened in 1838 as the northern terminus of the London and Birmingham Railway. There was also a connection with the Grand Junction Railway, whose line ran from Birmingham to Manchester and Liverpool, making the, then, town a railway 'hub' between London and the north-west of England. A dispute between the London and Birmingham Railway, who were negotiating with the Birmingham and Manchester Railway and were interested in using the independent Trent Valley Railway to avoid Birmingham and obtain a more direct route to the north-west, and the Grand Junction Railway, whose business would be threatened, led to the formation of the London and North Western Railway. Captain Mark Huish, secretary of the Grand Junction, had decided that the GJR should become a broad gauge line and negotiations began with the Great Western Railway, who were interested in bringing their 7 ft gauge into Birmingham via Oxford and Rugby. This move had so alarmed the London and Birmingham, who were the prime movers for the standardization of the 4 ft 8½ in gauge, that they called for deals with the GJR, and in 1846 the LNWR was formed with Mark Huish becoming General Manager. Once Huish had won, his interest in the GWR became hostile and the latter company had to find its own route into Birmingham. Curzon Street remained as the Birmingham terminus until New Street was opened in 1854. The station was used for a time by the Midland Railway until space could be found for them at New Street. Unlike the original London and Birmingham Railway station building at Euston, the one at Curzon Street has been preserved, even though it is in the middle of a goods yard.

The replacement for Curzon Street was New Street, designed by William Livlock and opened in 1854. The building was in a restrained Barry-esque style and the tracks were covered by a curved roof supported on thirty-six single span trussed cast iron arches weighing 25 tons each. In the distance is the passenger footbridge and a central carriage drive, known as Queens Drive, a public right of way which ran from the booking hall to Station Street. The station was shared by the LNWR and Midland Railway, both companies using platforms as required. Congestion soon became a problem, and in 1880 a new extension was added which became known as the Midland Extension because it gave that company its own platforms. The extension also cleared some of the worst slums in the town, making the area safer. On the right of this view are a pair of 2–4–2 Tanks, Nos 822 and 894, which appear to be on station pilot duties. A rake of LNWR express coaches can be seen just behind the signals in the centre of the picture.

New Street in its heyday before the First World War. There are several trains at the station, which seem to be locals as the motive power is in the form of 0–6–2 and 2–4–2 Tanks. On the left are goods wagons waiting for a train to arrive, while in the foreground is a small turntable, probably to turn railway wagons, which is operated by a horse, just visible on the left foreground. The station suffered bomb damage on the LNWR side during the Second World War which wrecked the overall roof on the original station, leaving the tracks open to the elements. The station was rebuilt in 1964.

LNWR 2–2–2–0 compound No. 311 *Rich Francis Roberts* blows off as it rests at New Street in 1903.

Ex-LNWR 4–4–0 'George V' class No. 5354 *New Zealand* waits at New Street with a north-bound train in the 1930s.

Express motive power typical of that seen at New Street in LNWR days is shown in this view taken on 16 July 1920. On the left is No. 514 *Puck*, a 'Jumbo' class 2–4–0, and on the right is No. 218 *Daphne*, a 4–4–0 of the 'Precursor' class. These, and several other LNWR types could be seen at New Street right up to the Second World War.

Ex-LNWR 0–6–2 Coal Tank No. 58900 passes through New Street station on 26 May 1951. The loco was probably on station pilot duties and would have been due for withdrawal in the next few years.

Waiting to take an excursion on the local branch lines in the Birmingham area, including the Halesowen branch, is ex-Midland Railway Johnson 0–6–0 No. 58271. The engine is on the LNWR side of the station and the effect of the bomb damage inflicted during the Second World War can be clearly seen.

Ex-Glasgow and South Western Railway side corridor Brake third-class carriage seen at New Street in 1955.

A railway coach with a long history at New Street in 1957. This coach originally belonged to the Great Central Railway, but was transferred to the Cheshire Lines Committee for use on their tracks between Chester and Liverpool. The coach was then absorbed into London Midland Region stock at nationalization.

Ex-LNWR 0–6–0 Coal engine No. 28619 heads a local train from New Street into the tunnel under the city centre as it heads towards Wolverhampton on 21 May 1948, during the first few months after nationalization. These engines could be seen on local trains in the years after the Second World War, until replaced by more modern BR 'Standard' class locos; these Coal engines then went for scrap.

The southern end of New Street station, with ex-LNWR 0–6–2 Coal Tank No. 46912 resting from her duties as station pilot. This scene was photographed on 5 June 1950, and an advertising hoarding showing an advert for 'Greys Cigarettes' can be clearly seen.

The signal-box and tunnels under the city at the southern end of New Street station in 1954. The buildings above the tunnels faced Worcester Street, which ran between Great Queen Street and the New Street junction with High Street, site of the famous Rotunda. On the far left of the picture is the front end of what seems to be a Stanier 'Black 5' 4–6–0 loco at the head of a London-bound train.

Rebuilding of New Street station commenced in 1964 as part of plans to electrify the London to Birmingham route. All London-bound traffic was transferred to Snow Hill while this work was undertaken. This view shows the south tunnel just after rebuilding had started.

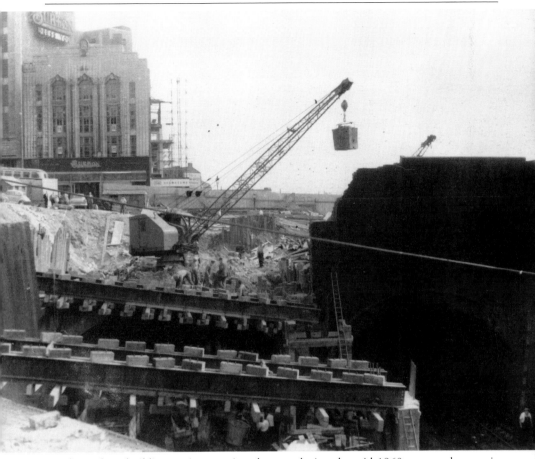

Work on the rebuilding project continued apace during the mid-1960s, as can be seen in this view of the reconstruction of the south tunnel seen here from Worcester Street. The new station was designed by the British Railways Architects Department and, when finished, became a twelve-platform structure covered by a seven acre concrete slab, favourite building material in the 1960s but not particularly attractive. The platforms were connected by escalators and stairs to a booking hall above. Above that were the shops of the Birmingham Shopping Centre, a covered shopping centre leading to the new Market Hall and Bull Ring centre. The modern Bull Ring lacks the charm of its predecessor, where barrow boys used to shout their wares from streets around St Martin's church.

The new south tunnel nearing completion. At the same time as this work was being undertaken, the rest of the city centre was being developed, making life rather difficult for
people shopping in the town. It has been suggested that shoppers are going to face these
problems all over again, as plans to redevelop the city centre are being proposed. These
include a new station at New Street which, if published plans are to be believed, will have
much more character than the present draughty structure.

Ex-Midland Railway 0–6–0 No. 3503 heads a local freight train past Monument Lane, the home of the LNWR locoshed serving New Street, on 3 July 1948. A local train of third-class non-corridor stock appears to be passing on the left. On the right is the signal-box with a rather unusual signal configuration just in front.

The north portal of Monument Lane tunnel seen from a local train.

Winson Green road bridge, carrying the A4040 road over the railway, looking towards Monument Lane in 1956.

The Stephenson's Locomotive Society ran a special excursion over the Harborne branch on 3 June 1950, the first passenger train on the line since November 1934. Ex-LNWR Webb 2–4–2 Tank No. 46757 is about to take the branch with its packed two-coach train. In its heyday the branch had a large number of passenger trains: the timetable for 1906 shows over fifty trains a day using the line. By the end of the First World War, however, the branch began to suffer from road competition in the shape of the electric tram which could operate a more direct service than the railway and was cheaper. Passenger numbers declined until, by 1934, there were insufficient passengers to make trains viable. The line retained freight traffic until 1950 when it closed altogether. The trackbed survives and is now a 'linear park'.

Icknield Port Road station, the first on the Harborne branch. The station looks rather gloomy in this view.

Hagley Road station, complete with staff, in its heyday. The number of adverts on the station suggests it was well used.

Terminus of the branch at Harborne. A local train, hauled by an LNWR 0–6–2 Tank engine, prepares to leave with a train for New Street.

Galton tunnel under the Oldbury road in 1955.

Smethwick station of the LNWR, one of three serving the town.

Spon Lane station in 1965, looking the worse for wear and showing signs of demolition.

Dudley station, on the jointly owned LNWR/GWR line. This view shows the LNWR side of the station.

Great Barr and Hamstead station with LNWR 0–8–0 No. 1012 on a mixed goods train. These engines were regularly seen in the Birmingham area where they were often used on heavy freight turns, hauling coal, iron, and steel between the coal mines and iron and steel works of the Black Country and Birmingham. The sheer quantity of freight traffic in this major industrial area produced huge profits for the LNWR and all the railway companies operating around Birmingham. It was this great industrial wealth and potential that attracted the railway companies to the town in the first place.

Handsworth Wood tunnel and cutting in the mid-1950s, before the line was electrified in the 1960s.

Ex-LNWR 'Claughton' 4–6–0 No. 5948 *Baltic* at Bescot on 18 August 1935. These engines were introduced in the final years of the LNWR, many operating in the Birmingham area including the First World War commemorative 'Claughton' LMS No. 5964 *Patriot*, which was rebuilt by the LMS to become the doyen of the famous 'Patriot' class engines.

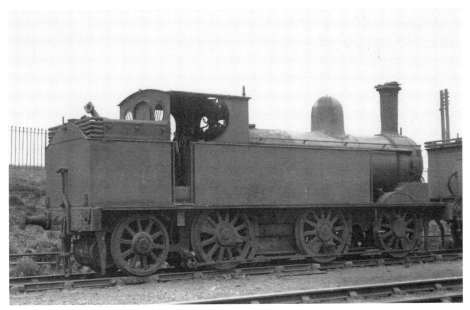

Unidentified ex-LNWR Coal Tank at Bescot on 9 May 1936.

A 2–2–2 engine hauls a train into Wednesbury in the late nineteenth century.

Wednesbury station in 1965, looking rather shabby.

Precursor to the railways as bulk carriers were the canals, many of the new railways in the Birmingham area following the course of canals already established. It is said that Birmingham has more miles of canal than Venice, although their location is somewhat less attractive. The line from New Street to Euston crosses the Birmingham Canal Navigations at Proof House junction and is seen from the canal itself in this view.

On the outskirts of Birmingham, on the route of the old London and Birmingham Railway Line, is the smart little station of Marston Green serving a picturesque little village. Another of the threats to rail travel exists nearby in the shape of the airport at Elmdon. In this view are the neat, wooden station buildings, unusual footbridge, and signal-box. It seems that early electrification work is underway, a gantry having been erected in the middle of the platform.

Another elegant station on the London route was at Hampton-in-Arden, seen here in 1950. The wooden buildings and awnings appear to be well cared for, something that is sadly lacking in these days of neglect of the railway system, and vandalism.

The Midland Railway

Perhaps the Midland Railway's chief claim to fame in the Birmingham area is that the company prevented the broad gauge interests of the GWR entering the standard gauge heartland of the LNWR by purchasing the Birmingham and Gloucester, and Gloucester and Bristol Railways from under their noses.

The Midland Railway's first Birmingham terminus was at Camp Hill, but the line was moved to Curzon Street until facilities were provided at New Street, from where the company operated until the 'grouping'. After becoming established at New Street, the Midland built a connecting line, and doubled the Birmingham West Suburban Railway, providing a shorter route to Bristol and a faster service to the west of England than the GWR could manage. The Camp Hill line lost its 'express' status and became a suburban line, its stations closing after the Second World War. Both lines remain open: the BWSR is the main line to the West Country and an important part of the 'Cross-City' railway service from Lichfield, on the old LNWR, to Longbridge, Barnt Green, and Redditch (all of which is to be electrified in 1993); the Camp Hill line is still important for freight traffic and as a relief line for express trains bypassing New Street.

Development of the Camp Hill and BWSR lines allowed the Midland to gain the advantage where passenger traffic was concerned, as new city suburbs were built at places like Bournville, Kings Norton and Northfield. There was, also, a substantial freight traffic serving the new industries that were springing up in that part of the city.

Some of the most famous express trains used Midland metals in Birmingham to reach their destinations. The *Devonian* ran from the Devon resorts to Leeds, calling at New Street, and the more famous *Pines Express* ran from Bournemouth to Manchester via the Somerset and Dorset Joint Railway. This train used the BWSR in the summer and the Camp Hill line, to avoid New Street, in the winter. The train was diverted to GWR metals after the S&DJR closed in 1966.

The Midland Line provided trains to the Lickey Hills, the playground for Birmingham families. The company's station at Barnt Green would often be packed with families waiting for trains home after a Sunday trip, providing much revenue for the railway. Barnt Green station remains open and is still used by people going to the 'Lickeys' for the day.

Saltley Motive Power Depot, the Midland Railway's main locomotive shed for Birmingham during the LMS period. In the centre is 2P 4–4–0 No. 699, one of the LMS-built examples of a design introduced as an express passenger locomotive by the Midland in 1912. The fireman is busy with coal on the tender while other members of the shed's staff attend to their duties. An ex-LNWR engine is visible on the left. Saltley was a round-house-type shed of the sort favoured by the Midland Railway, and was coded 3 in Midland days. At the 'grouping', in 1923, the shed was recoded 21A and this was retained until the end of its life. Under a modernization programme by British Railways in 1950, the shed was given a new roof, improving what had been unpleasant working conditions.

Ex-LMS 2P 4–4–0 in early BR numbering as 40745 outside Saltley shed. These engines were usefully employed on secondary and semi-fast trains in the Birmingham area.

Saltley shed in British Railways days on 29 April 1956. In the foreground is a 4F 0–6–0 No. 43523, a Midland design introduced by Sir Henry Fowler in 1911. The LMS went on to build 580 more of these useful freight engines for use all over their system. Other engines in this view include 3F and 2F 0–6–0 freight engines and ex-Lancashire and Yorkshire Railway designed Hughes-Fowler 2–6–0 'Crab' locomotives, so called because of the acute angle of the outside cylinders.

One of the Midland Railway's small 1F shunting tanks outside Saltley shed. This example, in early LMS livery and numbered 1669, did not survive into nationalization.

Another example of the ubiquitous 4F 0–6–0s at Saltley, on 30 April 1956. No. 43946 was one of those built by the Midland Railway in 1911.

A rear view of 4F 0–6–0 No. 43435 at Saltley on 15 September 1956. In the background is an ex-LMS 8F 2–8–0 heavy freight engine.

An ex-Midland Railway 1F 0–6–0 Tank engine, known as a 'half cab' because of the backless nature of the footplate, No. 41805 at Saltley in 1956. The engine's number is stencilled on the chimney, running plate, and buffer beam as well as the smokebox door; for what reason is unclear, for this was certainly unusual.

An unusual sight at Saltley was this American Pullman car body in use as a store some time in the mid-1950s. It would be intriguing to know what happened to this vehicle or whether it still exists.

Ex-LMS 4F No. 44413 0–6–0 heads south with a 'Down' freight past Landor Street junction. On the right is Saltley engine shed, with the concrete coaling tower in the background. To the left is the signal-box controlling Landor Street junction. The left-hand line is the ex-LNWR route to Bescot and Walsall, while the right-hand line heads towards Castle Bromwich and Water Orton.

An unidentified ex-LMS 'Jubilee' class 4–6–0 passes Landor Street in charge of a Bristol express.

Castle Bromwich station on the Midland Line to Water Orton. Sadly, the station no longer exists.

The Midland Railway gained access to New Street station by purchasing the Birmingham and Gloucester Railway from under the nose of the Great Western Railway, thus preventing the intrusion of the GWR broad gauge into the heart of the LNWR. Kirtley 2–2–2 No. 94A rests in the Midland extension of the station in the early 1890s.

The LNWR were grateful that the GWR had been prevented from bringing the broad gauge into New Street and welcomed the Midland Railway with alacrity. The last design of single wheelers, the M.R. Johnson 4–2–2, is seen at New Street, where No. 99 is at rest in 1903.

Johnson's 4–2–2 singles were largely rebuilt by his successor, Deely, and they survived well into the 1920s, hauling express and semi-fast trains. One of these rebuilds, No. 670, rests at New Street in the early 1920s.

A Johnson 4–4–0 No. 73 waits with a train at New Street at 3.05 p.m. one day in 1910.

A Kirtley 2–4–0 and a Johnson 'Spinner' 4–2–0, the name given to these single wheelers, wait at the western end of the Midland extension of New Street station with their respective expresses in 1910.

In the year before the 'grouping' Deely rebuilt Johnson 4–4–0 No. 506, classified 2P, here shown bringing a Bristol–Derby express into New Street.

Photographed during 1910, 0–4–4 Tank engine No. 1387 prepares to leave New Street station with a local train which will travel down the West Suburban Line to Kings Norton.

Midland Railway 4–4–0 No. 2606 waits at New Street, *c.* 1905.

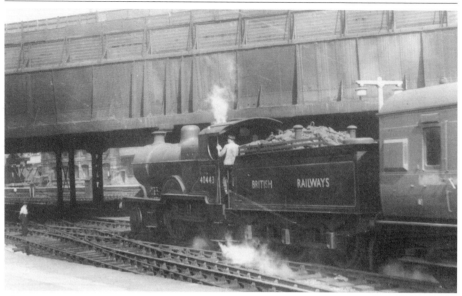

Photographed during early BR days, 2P 4–4–0 No. 40443, a Midland-built example, leaves New Street with a train for Bristol.

Despite bomb damage to New Street station, the overall roof on the Midland extension remained intact, giving a flavour of how the station used to look before the *Luftwaffe* inflicted so much damage. Waiting to depart with her train, ex-LMS 3-cylinder 'Compound' No. 41095 blows off under the overall roof on 5 June 1950.

A turn of the century view of Station Street, taken just outside the Midland extension of New Street station. Access to the station could be gained from Station Street, no doubt costing the railway company some loss of revenue.

A view from Birmingham Canal Navigations of the link between New Street and the Midland Railway's first main line into Birmingham at Camp Hill. This scene is near to Proof House junction, so named because the government gun-proofing house is nearby and the city was known for many years for its manufacture of guns.

A railway overbridge across the canal at Garrison Street. The line is the spur from Camp Hill to Proof House junction and the canal is the Birmingham and Warwick Junction Canal.

Sandy Lane, Bordesley, the point at which the Midland Railway's Camp Hill line and the Great Western Railway's line to Tyseley pass above the Grand Union Canal.

Garrison Lane locks at Brickyard Crossing. In the distance is the LNWR line to London, and the factory is the Morris Commercial van works at Adderley Park. In front is the Midland Line from Saltley to Camp Hill. The canal is the Birmingham and Warwick junction which connects Warwick Bar, Digbeth, with Salford Bridge at what is now the site of Spaghetti Junction. When the Midland Railway took over the Birmingham and Gloucester Line, trains were operated from a temporary terminus at Camp Hill, the line then proceeding through Moseley and Kings Heath to Kings Norton. The line was then extended to Curzon Street with the blessing of the LNWR until the Midland had access to New Street.

The Camp Hill line tunnel under the Coventry Road with the Coventry Road bus garage on the right. Just beyond the tunnel, the line enters a cutting below the St Andrews Ground, home of Birmingham City Football Club. There is a story that, in steam days, an old goods train used to pass behind the ground every Saturday afternoon while matches were in progress. Smoke from the engine would shroud the railway end of the ground, and if the Blues were attacking that end the ball would be in the back of the net when the smoke had cleared. Whether there is any truth in the story is open to question, but there is no doubt that the club has been somewhat less successful since steam disappeared from the line. Perhaps a steam excursion could be arranged in an effort to improve results?

The Classes of Trains shewn on this Table refer only to Stations between Worcester & Birmingham.	UP.				WEEKDAYS.									SUNDAYS.		
	1 2 GOV.	1 2 class	1 2 class	1 2 class	1 2 class	1 2 class	1 2 GOV.	1 2 GOV.	1 2 class					1 2 GOV.	1 2 GOV.	1 2 class
TRAINS LEAVE	a.m.	a.m.	a.m.	p.m.	p.m.	p.m.	p.m.	p.m.	p.m.					a.m.	p.m.	p.m.
OXFORD	..	..	..	8 28	11 40	2 40	..	..	6 50	..	..	..		..	4 35	..
Handboro'	..	..	..	8 50	11 55	8 5	..	..	7 15	..	..	..		..	5 0	..
Stratford	..	..	8 50	..	11 0	3 55	..	..	..	..	..	..		..	6 0	..
Evesham	..	..	9 30	10 10	1 42	4 35	..	..	8 25	..	..	..		..	6 40	..
Fladbury	..	..	9 37	..	1 50	4 42	..	..	..	..	..	..		..	6 47	..
Pershore	..	..	9 45	10 25	2 0	4 50	..	..	8 40	..	..	..		..	6 55	..
MALVERN	..	8 0	9 30	12 0	1 45	4 30	5 45	7 0	..	..	..	..		9 15	7 30	..
WORCESTER	7 48	9 38	10 17	2 5	4 35	5 20	7 10	7 35	9 27	..	..	..		9 50	8 20	9 27
Fearnal Heath	7 57	..	..	..	..	..	7 19	7 42	..	..	..	..		9 56	8 26	..
Droitwich	8 7	9 50	..	2 17	4 46	..	7 27	7 50	9 39	..	..	..		10 4	8 34	9 39
Stoke Works	8 19	10 0	..	..	4 55	..	7 37	8 1	..	..	..	..		10 14	8 44	..
Bromsgrove	8 31	10 12	10 43	2 36	5 5	5 44	7 47	8 13	9 56	..	..	..		10 24	8 54	9 56
Blackwell	8 38	..	..	2 42	5 11	..	7 53	8 20	..	..	..	..		10 31	9 1	..
Redditch { arr. dep.	9 5	10 55	..	3 10	5 45	..	8 15	..	..	..	..	..		10 55	9 25	..
	8 26	10 10	..	2 30	4 55	..	7 25	..	..	..	..	..		10 10	8 40	..
Barnt Green	8 45	10 27	..	2 49	5 17	..	7 58	8 25	..	..	..	..		10 37	9 7	..
King's Norton	8 57	10 37	..	..	5 29	..	8 6	8 38	..	..	..	..		10 48	9 18	..
Moseley	9 4	..	..	3 6	5 35	..	8 16	8 49	..	..	..	..		10 55	9 23	..
Camp Hill	9 11	..	..	..	..	..	8 21	8 55	..	..	..	..		11 0	9 30	..
BIRMINGHAM	9 25	11 0	11 20	3 25	5 55	6 20	8 35	9 10	10 30	..	..	..		11 15	9 45	10 30

BIRMINGHAM, to WORCESTER, MALVERN, STRATFORD, & OXFORD.

The Classes of Trains shewn on This Table refer only to Stations between Birmingham & Worcester.	DOWN				WEEKDAYS.									SUNDAYS.		
	1 2 class	1 2 GOV.	1 2 class	1 2 class	1 2 class	1 2 GOV.	1 2 class	1 2 class	1 2 GOV.					1 2 class	1 2 GOV.	1 2 GOV.
TRAINS LEAVE	a.m.	a.m.	a.m.	a.m.	p.m.	p.m.	p.m.	p.m.	p.m.					a.m.	a.m.	p.m.
BIRMINGHAM	2 45	7 5	9 15	10 0	1 35	3 30	4 25	4 50	7 10	..	..	..		2 45	6 45	5 0
Camp Hill	..	7 16	..	..	..	3 39	..	..	7 21	..	..	..		..	6 55	5 10
Moseley	..	7 23	..	10 14	..	3 45	..	5 5	7 27	..	..	..		..	7 1	5 15
King's Norton	..	7 30	..	10 22	..	3 52	..	5 12	7 34	..	..	..		..	7 9	5 22
Barnt Green	..	7 42	..	10 35	2 0	4 4	..	5 24	7 46	..	..	..		..	7 21	5 34
Redditch { arr. dep.	..	9 5	..	10 55	2 20	..	..	5 45	8 15	..	..	..		..	7 40	5 55
	..	7 48	..	10 10	1 40	..	..	4 55	7 25	..	..	..		..	7 0	5 10
Blackwell	..	7 48	..	10 41	2 6	4 9	..	..	7 53	..	..	..		..	7 27	5 39
Bromsgrove	3 18	7 59	9 47	10 52	2 16	4 20	5 4	5 43	8 6	..	..	..		3 18	7 38	5 49
Stoke Works	..	8 6	..	10 59	..	4 26	..	5 49	8 12	..	..	..		..	7 43	5 54
Droitwich	3 29	8 17	..	11 9	2 29	4 37	..	5 59	8 27	..	..	..		3 29	7 55	6 4
Fearnall Heath	..	8 23	..	..	..	4 45	..	..	8 36	..	..	..		..	8 3	6 12
WORCESTER	3 41	8 40	10 11	11 25	2 48	4 55	5 28	6 17	8 48	..	..	..		3 41	8 15	6 25
MALVERN	..	9 15	11 15	1 30	3 45	6 30	6 30	8 0	..	..	..	..		..	8 45	7 0
Pershore	..	..	10 55	1 10	..	5 25	..	9 5	9 5	..	..	..		..	10 40	6 35
Fladbury	..	..	11 2	1 17	..	5 33	..	9 12	9 12	..	..	..		..	10 47	6 42
Evesham	7 55	..	11 13	1 25	..	5 40	..	9 20	9 20	..	..	..		..	10 55	6 50
Stratford	..	..	12 5	..	..	6 25	..	..	..	..	..	..		..	11 40	7 35
Handborough	9 0	..	12 50	2 40	..	7 5	..	..	..	..	..	..		..	12 30	8 15
OXFORD	9 25	..	1 20	3 0	..	7 35	..	..	..	..	..	..		..	12 50	8 35

A pre-First World War timetable for the Midland Railway route via Camp Hill to Worcester, Stratford and Oxford. One interesting aspect of the timetable is the 'Government' trains, a throwback to the Gladstone Railway Act of 1844 which stated that third-class passengers had to be carried in proper accommodation.

Clifton Road railway bridge on the Camp Hill line in 1957. The bridge is unique in that the arch is square to the railway, whereas the road has to make a dog-leg turn to negotiate the bridge. There is no 'Low Bridge' warning for road traffic and the footpath is very narrow.

The railway tunnel at Moseley in 1955. This tunnel is reputed to be the first covered way.

Moseley station at the turn of the century, with a Midland Railway Bristol-bound express passing through. Express trains ceased operating along the branch when the Birmingham West Suburban Line opened to New Street, and suburban passenger traffic was suspended on 27 January 1941 as an economy measure. With no demand for a passenger service after the war, the line was abandoned in 1946 although it is still important for freight and as a relief passenger line when the BWSR is congested, particularly in the summer months. Moseley station suffered bomb damage during the blitz of 1940/1.

The station platform at Kings Heath in 1957 with its contingent of schoolboy train-spotters, a popular activity until dieselization seemed to drive them away.

Hazelwell station as it appeared after the line had closed to passengers. The canopy has become devoid of glass, but the building remains in good condition and retains its unusual chimneys and ornamental awning supports.

L M S

YOU CAN OBTAIN A

THIRD CLASS

Weekly Season Ticket

AVAILABLE FOR AN

UNLIMITED NUMBER OF JOURNEYS

COMMENCING APRIL 19th, 1925, TO

BIRMINGHAM

From the Stations shown below:

STATIONS.	Weekly Season Ticket Rate.		Cost per Day.	ROUTE.
	S.	D.	D.	
Penns	4	6	7¾	
Sutton Park ...	4	9	8¼	
Streatly	5	0	8¾	
Aldridge	5	0	8¾	
Selly Oak	2	2	3¾	
Bournville	2	9	4¾	Via Selly Oak
Camp Hill	1	10	3¼	
Brighton Road ...	2	0	3½	Via Camp Hill
Moseley	2	2	3¾	ditto
Kings Heath ...	2	8	4½	ditto
Hazelwell	3	1	5¼	ditto
Lifford	3	7	6¼	ditto
Lifford	4	0	7	Via Selly Oak or Camp Hill
*Kings Norton ...	4	0	7	Via Selly Oak
Kings Norton ...	4	3	7¼	Via Selly Oak or Camp Hill
*Northfield	4	6	7¾	Via Selly Oak
Northfield	4	10	8¼	Via Selly Oak or Camp Hill

* Not available via Camp Hill.

Tickets will be available from the Sunday to the following Saturday inclusive.

Get one Next Week. Save time, trouble and money.

No filling up of forms of application. Tickets obtained at the Booking Offices.

April, 1925. AD 161/2. H. G. BURGESS, General Manager.

An LMS advert for season tickets for passengers using the Camp Hill line and the West Suburban Line.

Holliday Street aqueduct, built by the Midland Railway to carry the Birmingham and Worcester Canal which had to be moved when the railway company extended the Birmingham West Suburban Line from its original terminus at Granville Street into New Street. This work was commenced in 1883 and completed in 1885. The line was doubled from the original single and brought up to a high standard. When opened, all expresses were transferred from the Camp Hill line to the shorter route. This aqueduct is a very attractive piece of Victoriana.

Suffolk Street tunnel seen from an approaching train, hauled in this instance by an ex-LMS 'Compound' 4–4–0, in 1956. This tunnel marks the spot where the New Street extension linked up with the original West Suburban Line.

Church Road junction, which featured a rather unusual signal. It was one of very few Midland signals which had the company's Wyvern crest entwined in the support bracket. The signal arm was made of wood and its balance weight was short enough to be clear of the station wall. It would be interesting to know whether any collector has this signal or whether it was scrapped, like so much of the old railway.

Suffolk Street tunnel seen from the junction with the goods depot at Suffolk Street itself.
Once the Midland Railway had built its New Street extension to the West Suburban Line,
the original terminus at Granville Street was extended under the Birmingham and
Worcester Canal to provide this goods depot which was kept busy until closure in the
1960s.

The first station after New Street on the BWSR was at Church Road, the site of which can be seen here, looking towards Five Ways. Just visible on the left is the Birmingham and Worcester Canal which the BWSR runs parallel with until it gets beyond Bournville.

Five Ways station, with the line to the goods depot in the background. The station closed in the 1960s, only to reopen as part of the West Midlands Passenger Transport Executive's plan to create the 'Cross-City' service between Lichfield, Longbridge (for which a new station was built) and Redditch. So successful has it been, that it is now the busiest passenger line outside London.

A rare Midland Railway concrete post signal near Selly Oak, which probably dates from the First World War. Selly Oak was the home of the Ariel Motor Cycle Company whose products, along with those of other manufacturers in the city, brought cheap personal transport to the ordinary working man. A motor cycle could be bought for less than £25 in the 1930s, and sowed the seeds for the decline of railways in Britain.

Bournville station before the First World War. This was the fourth name carried by the station. When the line was opened, in 1876, the station was named Stirchley Street. The Cadbury family built their chocolate factory here in 1879 and named the area Bournville. This new name was incorporated into the station name in 1880, when it was retitled Stirchley Street and Bournville. As the works become increasingly important the station was renamed again to Bournville and Stirchley Street in 1888. In April 1904 Stirchley Street was dropped altogether. When the BWSR first opened the line turned off at Bournville and joined the Camp Hill line at Lifford. In 1885 a more direct line to Kings Norton was opened and the line to Lifford became a short branch. It did, however, allow the Midland Railway to run a circular service using the BWSR and the Camp Hill line.

Bournville station with Cadbury's chocolate factory in the background. The Bournville village was established by the Cadbury brothers at the turn of the century, and was an example of high quality accommodation for working-class families and the epitome of the 'Garden Village'. Such was the interest engendered in this project that people came from all over the UK to see it – not least among them King George V, who came in 1919 – many arriving by train. The works was also opened to the public in the 1930s and special train excursions were run to Bournville for such visits, making the station a very important place.

An early twentieth-century advert for the products of the famous chocolate works at Bournville.

Bournville had its own locoshed, opened in 1895, to deal with the increased traffic demands caused by the opening of the BWSR. It was a subshed of Saltley and coded 3A in Midland days. It became 21B after the 'grouping' in 1935 and had a life of sixty-five years. The shed became a backwater in the 1930s, housing some ancient locomotives of the old railway company. As such, it became a magnet for railway enthusiasts who could find many old types that were long since gone from the rest of the LMS system. One such example can be seen here, a very picturesque double-framed Kirtley 0–6–0 engine No. 22834 of nineteenth-century vintage resting inside the roundhouse type shed on 2 March 1935. The shed was never modernized right up to closure and the site is now occupied by modern industrial units. The last engine off shed, when it was closed on 14 February 1960, was 'Black 5' 4–6–0 No. 44843.

The home signal at Bournville, with the locoshed in the background. In the foreground is the old branch to Lifford.

Another view of the home signal, with the locoshed on the left and Bournville signal-box in the centre background. The chimney in the distance has the legend 'Join the Co-op' and is probably the site of the Co-op dairy in nearby Stirchley.

A home signal on the old Lifford branch. The original line between Lifford and Bournville is somewhat overgrown in this 1956 view.

Lifford curve passing under the Pershore Road bridge, Cotteridge in 1956. The curve here was rather tight as the check rails indicate.

The northern end of Kings Norton station, showing the island platform built when the line was quadrupled in the 1920s. The Camp Hill line is in the foreground and the BWSR is just visible on the left. The island platform was a favourite spot for schoolboy train-spotters in the days of steam. I have fond memories of watching the *Devonian*, usually 'Jubilee'-hauled, running through the station at speed, as well as the great variety of ex-LMS and BR steam engines hauling Bristol-bound trains through the station.

Kings Norton station in the days before the Midland main line was quadrupled. The left-hand platform became an island, with new buildings replacing those in view, and the gardens beyond were lost to make way for additional tracks and a new platform. The building on the right-hand platform still exists, although in a somewhat dilapidated condition, while the island-platform building has been demolished, leaving the station with a somewhat spartan appearance. There are new structures on the station, built as part of 'Cross-City' development, but they are only at the northern end of the station and are very simple structures. I was on Kings Norton station quite recently and was saddened to see how much the place had changed.

There were substantial carriage sidings just beyond the southern end of Kings Norton station which were later to become storage areas for newly manufactured cars from the Austin works at Longbridge. The sidings are still there and are being used as the central depot in connection with the electrification of the whole of the 'Cross-City' line, due to be completed in 1993. This 1956 view shows an ex-Midland Railway saloon, built in 1910 and used for disinfecting purposes.

The railway overbridge carrying the Midland main line over the road close to the island-platformed Northfield station.

The Midland Birmingham–Bristol main line at Halesowen junction, with a south-bound passenger train approaching in July 1915. The locality is now the site of a new Longbridge station, built as part of the 'Cross-City' service to replace the original station situated in the middle of the Austin works on the old Halesowen branch.

The signal-box at Longbridge on the Halesowen branch. This is now used by the Austin works to control its private railway but was once at the entrance to Longbridge railway station. The line was jointly owned by the Midland and Great Western Railways and linked the Black Country with the Midland's Bristol main line. The line closed to passengers in 1919 but was used for freight to the Austin works and for workmen's trains which were withdrawn in 1958. The line closed in 1964 when the land was taken from the construction of a bypass road and the M5 motorway.

The remains of Rubery station in 1956, complete with passing loop and signal-box. The signal is of interest: it is a Midland post with a GWR signal arm.

A double distant signal on the Halesowen branch near Rubery in the mid-1950s.

GWR 0–6–0 Pannier Tank No. 2718 with a passenger train near Rubery on 12 July 1935. The train was taking workers to the Austin factory from Halesowen. The loco itself was originally built at Wolverhampton as a saddle tank and converted some years later.

Another works train, hauled by GWR 0–6–0 Pannier Tank No. 2719, nears Rubery on 29 May 1935.

Haden Hill tunnel on the Halesowen branch in 1955. The distorted portal was a feature of the tunnel and had been in this condition for some years.

Double distant signal at Rubery.

Double-framed Kirtley 0–6–0 No. 22852, probably of Bournville shed, hauls a freight past Rubery on 29 May 1935.

Distant signal near Hunnington in 1956. Hunnington is the site of the Blue Bird toffee factory.

Dowery Dell viaduct, between Rubery and Halesowen, in 1939. There was a weight limit on the viaduct and no locos heavier than power class 2F could be allowed along the Halesowen branch. This weight limit ensured that the line was usually operated by engines of pre-'grouping' vintage, the Midland types being shedded at Bournville.

Terminus of the branch at Halesowen. The wooden station building can be seen in this pre-Second World War view.

Halesowen station on 30 May 1959. An excursion run by the Stephenson's Locomotive Society has just terminated. The engines in this view are ex-Midland 2Fs Nos 58271 and 58147.

Back on the main Birmingham–Bristol line, with the south end of Cofton tunnel in view, in July 1915. When the line was quadrupled the tunnel was demolished.

Demolition of Cofton tunnel, to make way for extra railway tracks, in progress in April 1928.

Hughes-Fowler 'Crab' 2–6–0 No. 42857 pilots ex-Midland Compound 4–4–0 No. 41078 with a local train on the Bristol main line into Barnt Green station on 15 September 1956. The line on the left is the branch to Alvechurch and Redditch. Barnt Green is the gateway to the Birmingham playground of the Lickey Hills, and on summer Sundays the station would be crowded with people awaiting trains.

REDDITCH BRANCH—REDDITCH TO BARNT GREEN.

	WEEK DAYS.						SUNDAYS.			
	1 2 gov.	1 2 gov.	1 2 gov.	1 2 gov.	1 2 gov.	1 2 gov.	1 2 gov.	1 2 gov.	1 2 gov.	1 2 gov.
	a.m.	a.m.	p.m.	p.m.	p.m.	p.m.	a.m.	a.m.	p.m.	p.m.
Redditch ....dep.	8 25	10 10	1 40	2 30	4 55	7 25	7 0	10 10	5 10	8 40
Alvechurch .... „	8 34	10 19	1 49	2 39	5 4	7 34	7 9	10 19	5 19	8 49
Barnt Green............arr.	8 40	10 25	1 55	2 45	5 10	7 40	7 15	10 25	5 25	8 55
Birmingham ....arr.	9 25	11 0	..	3 25	5 55	8 35	..	11 15	..	9 45

REDDITCH BRANCH—BARNT GREEN TO REDDITCH.

	WEEK DAYS.						SUNDAYS.			
	1 2 gov.	1 2 gov.	1 2 gov.	1 2 gov.	1 2 gov.	1 2 gov.	1 2 gov.	1 2 gov.	1 2 gov.	1 2 gov.
	a.m.	a.m.	p.m.	p.m.	p.m.	p.m.	a.m.	a.m.	p.m.	p.m.
Birmingham ....dep.	7 5	10 0	1 35	..	4 50	7 10	6 45	..	5 0	..
Barnt Green ....„	8 50	10 40	2 5	2 55	5 30	8 0	7 25	10 40	5 40	9 10
Alvechurch ....„	8 56	10 46	2 11	3 1	5 36	8 6	7 31	10 46	5 46	9 16
Redditch ....arr.	9 5	10 55	2 20	3 10	5 45	8 15	7 40	10 55	5 55	9 25

A Midland Railway timetable for the Redditch branch.

Barnt Green in 1957, showing the railway bridge carrying the Redditch branch over the road. It is interesting to note that there is very little traffic on the road, something that will change in the next twenty years or so thanks to the products of the nearby Longbridge factory.

A very attractive picture of Alvechurch station in 1956. The station is situated on the Redditch branch and is about a mile away from the village itself. Despite loss of traffic in the 1960s and threat of closure, the line remains open and has experienced an upsurge in traffic since the 'Cross-City' services began to operate and the town of Redditch was greatly enlarged by new housing development.

An unidentified Midland Railway 2–4–0 on an 'Up' passenger train climbs the Lickey Incline with an 0–6–0 Tank providing banking assistance. The Lickey Incline is probably one of the most famous banks in Britain, with its two-mile climb at 1 in 37, and has, no doubt, been cursed by many a fireman who has tried to maintain steam as his engine climbed.

Ex-Midland Railway 2P 4–4–0 No. 715 on the Lickey Incline on 29 May 1935. Introduction of diesel-electric motive power on the main line did make the climb less difficult for engine crews, although the first diesels were still banked in the late 1950s. Modern high-speed trains take the bank as though it didn't exist; how the old firemen would have appreciated that.

Ex-LMS 'Patriot' class 4–6–0 No. 45506 *The Royal Pioneer Corps* heads a York–Bristol express at Blackwell, at the top of the Lickey Incline, in 1956. Bristol-bound trains ran down the bank from here.

Ex-LMS 'Jubilee' class 4–6–0 No. 45577 *Bengal* climbs the Lickey Incline with an 'Up' relief train.

Hughes-Fowler 'Crab' 2–6–0 No. 42846 reaches the top of the bank with an 'Up' local train.

A Stanier 2–6–0 reaches the top of the bank with a relief train.

Ex-LMS 4F 0–6–0 No. 44187 brings a train of coal wagons up the Lickey bank with assistance provided at the rear. This view was taken on 5 June 1950.

BR 'Standard' class 4 4–6–0 climbs the bank with a three-coach local in 1957. The train was banked by an ex-GWR Pannier Tank 0–6–0 No. 8402. The train load seems too light to require banking assistance, but a banker was put on to prevent breakaways.

British Railways were keen to see if the Lickey Incline could be climbed without the use of banking engines, and they conducted experiments using a 'Black 5' 4–6–0 No. 44176 and a special inspection saloon on 6 March 1955. It would appear to have been a failure as bankers were used right up until the end of steam.

Ex-Midland Railway Inspection Saloon used on the special Lickey Incline trials of 6 March 1956.

To cope with the demands of the Lickey Incline, the Midland Railway introduced its largest, and specially built engine, to the line. The famous Lickey Banker was an 0–10–0 built at Derby in 1910. The engine is seen here in original Midland Railway condition as number 2290 at Blackwell in 1922, a few months before the 'Grouping'.

The Lickey Banker in May 1948 at Bromsgrove.

The Lickey Banker in BR days as 58100 awaiting its turn of duty at Bromsgrove on 26 May 1951. The engine was withdrawn in 1956.

A quartet of ex-LMS 'Jinty' 0–6–0 Tank engines descend the Lickey Incline after giving banking assistance in June 1950. This was not an unusual sight in steam days as more than one small engine was required to lift heavy trains over the bank.

'Crab' 2–6–0 on a fitted freight at Bromsgrove just before attempting the bank.

LMS 'Jinty' 0–6–0 Tank No. 7115 shunts in the station yard at Bromsgrove on 2 March 1935. Bromsgrove was the home of banking engines used on Lickey Incline, being situated at the bottom of the bank.

Ex-Midland Compound 4–4–0 No. 41058 pauses at Bromsgrove station with a local train for Birmingham on 26 May 1951.

Lickey bankers at rest in Bromsgrove. Replacement for the old Midland 0–10–0 was a 9F 2–10–0 seen here. A Beyer-Garratt from the old LNER was tried on the bank but with only moderate success. The other engine is an 0–6–0 Pannier Tank. This scene was taken in January 1957.

Following nationalization, the Lickey Incline was transferred to the Western Region, a certain irony after all those years of Midland and LMS ownership when the GWR wanted it in the first place. However, motive power using the Lickey was usually of types that once belonged to the LMS and Midland Railways. The Western Region did, however, introduce ex-GWR locomotives to Bromsgrove for banking duties up the Lickey Incline, operating alongside old LMS types. Here ex-GWR 2–8–0 Tank No. 5226 drops off the rear of the train it has banked up to Blackwell on 26 September 1959.

Ex-GWR 0–6–0 Pannier Tank No. 8404 runs down the incline after banking a train on 22 April 1958.

Another ex-GWR locomotive, 2–8–0 Tank No. 5226, runs back down the bank to Bromsgrove after assisting a train up the incline. The headcode is wrong for a light engine.

Bromsgrove 'Down' station platform buildings as they were in 1959, with a wagon works to the right, behind the fence. The locomotive passing through, light, is ex-LMS 2P 4–4–0 returning to Bath after overhaul at Derby. This engine was originally LMS No. 576 and was subsequently 'sold' to the Somerset and Dorset Joint Railway to become their No. 45 and was painted in S&DJR blue. In 1930 the engine was returned to the LMS and renumbered 634, becoming 40634 when the LMS was nationalized.

SECTION THREE

The Great Western Railway

Whatever the status of the GWR among railway fans, the company was something of a 'Cinderella' in Birmingham. Its express routes to London and the West Country tended to take more circuitous directions than its rivals. Even when a more direct route to London, the Great Western/Great Central Joint Line from Bicester to Northolt (opened in 1906), cut the time from Birmingham to London to a more competitive two hours, the LNWR was more established and associated with trips to London so they lost little traffic. Only when New Street was closed for electrification work did Snow Hill really benefit from London traffic, but this was short lived and as soon as work on New Street was complete virtually all London trains become electric-hauled to Euston.

The Midland Railway had the more direct route to the West Country, and the GWR tried to compete by opening the North Warwickshire Line to Stratford-upon-Avon to connect with lines to Honeybourne and Cheltenham, creating a shorter link with the West Country. Apart from summer season traffic, the GWR could not attract the passenger numbers of the Midland.

Expresses no longer use the old GWR main line to Paddington; they run from New Street to Coventry (on the old LNWR route) and then via Kenilworth to meet the old GWR main line at Leamington Spa. West Country services use the Midland main line to Bristol, leaving the North Warwickshire Line for suburban traffic only. This perhaps more than anything reveals the secondary status of the GWR in Birmingham.

In spite of the company's 'Cinderella' status, it could boast two main line stations, Snow Hill and Moor Street. Snow Hill was the main station, and a very clean and 'classy' place it was, as befits all that was good about the GWR, it was never as 'brash' as New Street. Moor Street was a terminus station built to relieve the rather cramped main station and to deal with the many suburban services from Leamington Spa, on the main London line, and Stratford-upon-Avon. Some excursion trains also called there in the summer months when Snow Hill could not cope. Both stations were closed, Snow Hill in 1972 and Moor Street in 1987, only to be replaced by new ones of the same name as roads have become so congested that people are looking to the railways again to solve their travel problems, a tribute, perhaps, to the foresight of railway builders of the nineteenth century.

Great Western 2–4–0 No. 214 rests with a train at Wednesbury station around 1904. The station footbridge, on the left, is a typical GWR covered station bridge, common at most of that company's stations.

Stourbridge junction locoshed on 24 April 1932, with 'Aberdare' class 2–6–0 No. 2615 at the front of a rake of GWR Tank locos, an 0–6–0 Pannier Tank and a pair of 2–6–2 Prairie Tanks. The 'Aberdare' engines were unusual double-framed freight engines introduced in the latter years of the nineteenth century to handle South Wales coal traffic, hence their nicknames. They were reboilered by Churchward in the early years of this century, and a few survived to enter BR ownership.

Passing Stourbridge junction with a Worcester–Birmingham train is double-framed Churchward 4–4–0 No. 3444 *Cormorant*. The GWR was unique in that it was building double-framed engines well into this century. A double-framed 4–4–0 of the 'Atbara' class, the famous *City of Truro*, very similar to this engine, was reputed to have been the first loco to achieve 100 m.p.h. with the Plymouth–London mail train in 1904.

Dudley station in the years prior to the Second World War. In this view are a pair of local trains, the nearest a railmotor service with an 0–6–0 Pannier Tank in charge. In the background is another local hauled by a 2–6–2 Prairie Tank.

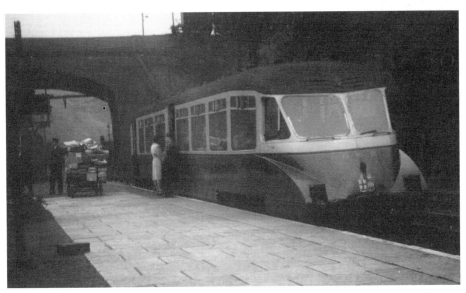

Forerunner of the modern diesel railcars were these single diesel units introduced by the GWR in the 1930s for local traffic and seen here at Dudley. These vehicles were built by AEC and fitted with Park Royal bodies. They were very well received and some lasted into the 1950s.

Hauling a mixed freight train through the Black Country is ex-GWR 'Grange' class loco No. 6848 *Toddington Grange*, one of the many GWR 4–6–0 mixed-traffic engines.

Handsworth and Smethwick station, on the line between Snow Hill and Swan Village in the heart of the Black Country, seen here in the 1950s.

BIRMINGHAM AND SWAN VILLAGE.   151

		Week Days.								M				M						M		
		a.m.	a.m.		a.m.	a.m.	a.m.	a.m.	a.m.	a.m.	a.m.	a.m.	a.m.	a.m.	a.m.	a.m.	a.m.	a.m.	a.m.	a.m.	a.m.	
...ingham (Snow Hill) ... dep		5 35	5 40	...	6 25	6 30	6 55	7 20	7 40	7 46	8 5	8 20	8 43	8 45	8 55	9 30	9 50	10 10	10 25	...	10 42	...
...ey		5 39	5 44		6 29	6 34	6 50	7 24	.	7 49	8 9		.	8 48	8 59	.	9 54	10 14	.			
...nd Winson Green		.	5 47	.	6 33	6 37	7 2	7 27	..	7 52	8 12	...	8 51	9 2		.						
...worth and Smethwick		5 45	5 53	...	6 38	6 41	7 6	7 32	7 46	7 57	8 16		8 50	8 55	9 6	9 37	9 59	10 19	10 31	...	10 48	...
...Bromwich		5 50				6 47			7 51	8 2		8 21	8 55	9 2		9 44		10 24	10 37	...		
...n Village ... arr.		5 54				6 51			7 54	8 6			9 0	9 6				10 28	10 40			

A GWR timetable for services between Snow Hill and Swan Village.

The GWR main line between Hockley and Handsworth, near Soho, on the Snow Hill–Wolverhampton section, with a train coming into view.

Hockley No. 2 tunnel in 1958 with five tracks running through – four running lines and a siding. The signal-box controlling the tunnel can be seen in the distance. A large goods yard was situated at Hockley to deal with goods traffic for Birmingham.

A smokey view of Hockley No. 1 tunnel in 1958.

An ex-GWR 53XX class 2–6–0 loco on a Saturday relief train about to enter Hockley No. 1 tunnel in 1955. This view was taken from a train running alongside. It is said that trains often used to race each other on the parallel tracks through the tunnel.

A 1956 view of Hockley No. 1 tunnel from the rear of a train.

Hockley No. 2 tunnel after Snow Hill station was closed, with tracks remaining in situ but about to be removed. Snow Hill ceased to be a main line station in 1967, but was retained for suburban use until 1972 when it closed altogether and all track was lifted.

Hockley No. 2 tunnel with track-lifting work nearly complete.

Hockley Cutting with Livery Street bridge in the background. The decline of the GWR route is evident here, but there is now hope that the line may reopen as part of a scheme to link Stourbridge with Stratford-upon-Avon and Leamington, via a new Snow Hill which was opened in 1987.

Hockely Cutting in 1974, with the removal of the track to Wolverhampton virtually complete, a symbol of the triumph of the electrified LNWR route over that of the GWR.

In happier times GWR 'Hall' class 4–6–0 locomotive No. 4933 *Hewlett Hall* brings a four-coach train from Wolverhampton into Snow Hill in the 1930s.

Thwarted by the LNWR and the Midland Railway in its attempts to bring trains into Birmingham, the GWR had to seek an alternative route. The company achieved this when they absorbed the Oxford and Birmingham Railway in the 1850s. The company had a small station at Snow Hill which had been opened in 1852 as a modest wooden structure. This building was removed to Didcot when the GWR built a more substantial station in 1871, the building seen in this view pictured from Livery Street at the turn of the century. This station lasted until a new structure, and the one best known in the city, was commenced in 1906. The Great Western Hotel, which fronted the station, was built in 1863 and was designed by J.A. Chatwin. The hotel was taken over for offices when the final station was completed and the ground floor became a restaurant.

A Dudley local train waits at Snow Hill with an 0–4–2 Tank engine in charge in 1955.

Another Dudley train at Snow Hill, this time made up of two coaches, probably in preparation for the rush hour.

Snow Hill station in 1958, with the largest of the GWR express engines, 'King' class 4–6–0 No. 6010 *King Charles I*, on the 'Up' 'Cambrian Coast Express'. The 'King' would have been put on at Shrewsbury, replacing a 'Manor' lightweight 4–6–0 which was used on this train as it ran along the Cambrian Coast line. The only clean engine I ever saw in my days as a train-spotter was one of this class, one summer afternoon at Snow Hill, and what a magnificent sight she made. It would have been around 1960, and she was probably newly outshopped from Swindon works, perhaps her last overhaul before scrapping as most of this class had gone by 1963. Snow Hill was popular at the start of summer holidays and could be extremely busy at the peak of the season, but it became most busy when New Street was closed for rebuilding and electrification work in 1963 and all London services were transferred to Snow Hill. When work on New Street was finished all London traffic was removed back for electric operation and Snow Hill was closed to all main-line traffic in 1967, the end signalled by the haulage of a special steam excursion on 6 March 1967. As preserved loco 7029 *Clun Castle* hauled out empty carriage stock that evening, the curtain came down on over a century of express trains from Snow Hill.

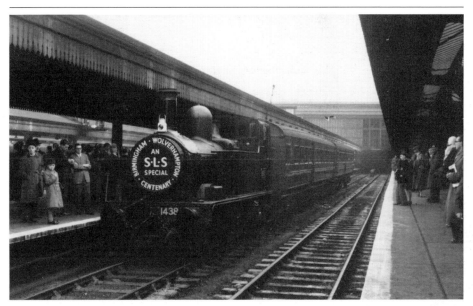

An SLS special excursion from Wolverhampton to Snow Hill, hauled by an 0–4–2 Tank, waits at Snow Hill on 13 November 1954.

A Dean 4-wheel coach, in Departmental use, rests adjacent to No. 12 platform, Snow Hill in 1956.

The south portral of Snow Hill tunnel a few years after the station closed. If ever there was a symbol of the decline of one of the great Birmingham stations, it is this. Only the trackbed and the sign warning of catchpoints give some indication that this was once an important railway line. The loss of Snow Hill was mourned by many and they felt that the decision to close was rather hasty, arguing that New Street would not be able to cope with the extra traffic. Their opinions have been partly vindicated for Snow Hill has reopened, albeit as a suburban station under an office block.

Despite the GWR's minor status as far as its express services in Birmingham were concerned, their suburban trains did serve some well-heeled areas in and around the city and made the company money. Snow Hill was rather cramped and had difficulty coping with this traffic from the south. To cope, the GWR built a new station in 1909. The station was a terminus and was fitted with an electrically operated traverser which could take engines up to the size of a 'Castle' and release them from their trains. The station dealt not only with suburban traffic, but excursion trains that could not be handled at Snow Hill were terminated at Moor Street. In this view, a typical suburban train is at one of the platforms and a Prairie 2–6–2 Tank loco, used on these services, can be seen to the left. On the extreme left is the Moor Street Goods Depot, with the line to Snow Hill behind the fence on the right.

Number 2 platform, Moor Street in 1957, with a suburban train just arrived. There are adverts for holiday destinations in North Wales and Devon on the station concourse.

An ex-Glasgow and South Western Railway 6-wheel passenger brake van, in use for checking weighing machines, at Moor Street Goods Yard in 1961.

Bordesley station, with a GWR 'Mogul' 2-6-0 running through with a train of oil tankers, looking the worse for wear. Bordesley was always a bleak-looking place, but it was close to the Coventry and Stratford Roads where there was much industry, and was useful for access to Birmingham City's football ground. There were once cattle pens here where cattle would be unloaded for the nearby market. The overbridge in the distance carries the Midland Railway's Camp Hill line over the GWR.

Small Heath station, close to where the BSA once had a motor cycle factory in Golden Hillock Road. BSA started out making guns, but turned to bicycles and motorbikes in later years. The factory suffered severe bomb damage during the last war, with great loss of life, and closed down in the 1970s, sending shock waves through the whole of the motor industry.

Tyseley station is a junction of lines to London (Paddington), via Solihull and Leamington Spa, with the North Warwickshire Line to Stratford-upon-Avon. The Paddington line has been reduced to a suburban branch as London trains now run from New Street via Coventry. The North Warwickshire Line was scheduled for closure under the Beeching proposals, but remains open thanks to the efforts of the North Warwick Line Action Committee.

A 'Hall' class 4–6–0 passes through Tyseley with a train from Oxford after leaving the North Warwickshire Line.

Tyseley had carriage sidings and a locoshed supplying rolling stock and locomotives for Birmingham services. An unusual item of rolling stock on the carriage sidings was this ex-Barry Railway railcar trailer photographed in 1951.

A broadside view of the ex-Barry Railway railcar trailer in the carriage sidings.

Engineers Tool Van No. W71 on the sidings at Tyseley.

The bracket signal at Tyseley, complete with telegraph insulators on the post.

The locoshed at Tyseley in 1957, with four 2–6–2 Prairie Tank locos in view. Tyseley shed was opened in 1908 and was an important workshop. Just before nationalization it was home to some 118 locos, from small tank engines for local use to large express engines. The shed was closed by BR in 1969 and its buildings demolished, leaving one turntable open to the elements. In the same year the site was taken over by the newly formed Birmingham Railway Museum with financial support from the City Council. The museum became home to newly preserved 'Castle' 4–6–0 *Clun Castle* and ex-LMS 'Jubilee' class 4–6–0 *Kohlapur*, along with numerous tank engines and items of rolling stock. The museum grew in status, operating main-line steam excursions and servicing locos from other main-line trips as well as attracting enthusiasts to the museum itself. There were plans to rebuild the old shed, but withdrawal of financial support from the City Council in 1989 left the museum with financial problems. It survives today, despite its difficulties, and still attracts visitors to view the collection.

Acocks Green station in 1905. This was the first station at Acocks Green which, when built, served a relatively rural population. The area expanded greatly in the early years of this century, and the number of waiting passengers bears testament to that. Approaching the station is a local train for Birmingham hauled by a 517 class 0–4–2 Tank.

Week Days.

Miles			a.m.	a.m.	a.m.		a.m.	a.m.	a.m.	a.m.	a.m.	M		a.m.					M	T	M	a.m.	a.m.
	Birmingham { Snow Hill	dep.	5 40	6 35			7 0	7 18	7 35	7 40		8 5	8 32			9 3				9 44		10 25
	{ Moor Street	,,			6 55						7 45					9 10			10 5		
1¼	Bordesley	,,	5 43	6 39	6 58		7 4	7 23	7 38	7 44	7 48	8 9	8 36			9 7	9 13	9 49	10 8	10 29
2¼	Small Heath and Sparkbrook	,,	5 47	6 43	7 2		7 8	7 29	7 42	7 48	7 52	8 13	8 40			9 11	9 17	10 12	10 34
3½	Tyseley	,,	5 50	6 47	7 6		7 11	7 35	7 45	7 51	7 54	8 16	8 43			9 14	9 19	10 14	10 37
4½	Acock's Green and South Yardley	arr.	5 54	6 51	7 10		7 15	7 40		7 55		8 19	8 47			9 17				10 40

			M		S	M			p.m.	p.m.	p.m.	G	M	S	M-M	G	G	S	S	M
Birmingham { Snow Hill	dep.		a.m.	a.m.	a.m.	p.m.	p.m.	12 45			12 58		1 6	1 13	1 36	1 50	2 5	2 10	2 30
{ Moor Street	,,		10 30	11 25	12 5		12 25		12 48		12 55		1 0		1 20				2 35
Bordesley	,,		10 33	11 29	12 9	12 25	12 51		12 57	1 3	1 9	1 17	1 23	1 53	1 55	2 9	2 14	2 33	2 38
Small Heath and Sparkbrook	,,		10 37	11 34	12 13	12 29	12 55		1 1	1 7	1 13	1 21	1 27	1 56	1 59	2 12	2 36	2 46
Tyseley	,,		10 39	11 39	12 18	12 34	12 58		1 5	1 9	1 16	1 26	1 29	1 42	2 15	2 39	2 48
Acock's Green and South Yardley	arr.		11 48	12 23	12 53	1 1		1 9		1 20	1 30			1 45	2 18	2 52

			M			M		G	S	M	G	G		M	G	G		M
Birmingham { Snow Hill	dep.	3 0	3 50		4 35		p.m.	5 10	5 30		5 15	5 35		5 55	6 5		6 7		6 30
{ Moor Street	,,			4 20			5 6					5 40				6 7
Bordesley	,,	3 4	3 53	4 23	4 39		5 8	5 14	5 14	5 15	5 19	5 58	5 46	5 58		6 11	6 13	6 34
Small Heath and Sparkbrook	,,	3 12	3 57	4 27	4 43			5 18	5 19	5 23	5 42	5 47		6 15	6 17
Tyseley	,,	3 16	4 0	4 29	4 46			5 21	5 21	5 26	5 44	5 51		6 15	6 19	6 19
Acock's Green and South Yardley	arr.	3 20	4 3		4 49			5 25		5 29		5 54		6 11		6 23

			S	G	M		G				p.m.	M		M		M		
Birmingham { Snow Hill	dep.	6 30	6 35		6 50		7 10	7 30			8 10		8 50	9 20	9 35		10 29	11 0
{ Moor Street	,,					6 45		7 5			7 40	8 45			10 10
Bordesley	,,	6 34	6 40	6 42	6 55		7 14	7 34		7 43	8 14	8 48	8 54	9 23	9 39	10 13	10 24	11 4
Small Heath and Sparkbrook	,,	6 39	6 44	6 47	7 0		7 18	7 38		7 47	8 18	8 52	8 58	9 27	9 43	10 17	10 28	11 8
Tyseley	,,	6 43	6 48	6 49	7 4	7 11	7 21	7 41		7 49	8 21	8 54	9 2	9 47	10 19	10 31	11 11
Acock's Green and South Yardley	arr.	6 47	6 52		7 8		7 25	7 45		8 25		9 6		9 51	10 34	11 15

Sundays.

		a.m.	a.m.	a.m.	p.m.	p.m.	p.m.	p.m.	p.m.	p.m.
Birmingham { Snow Hill	dep.	7 45	9 15	10 30	12 50	2 0	3 20	5 10	7 15	8 32
{ Moor Street	,,									
Bordesley	,,	7 49	9 19	10 34	12 54	2 4	3 24	5 14	7 19	8 36
Small Heath and Sparkbrook	,,	7 53	9 23	10 38	12 58	2 10	3 28	5 18	7 23	8 40
Tyseley	,,	7 55	9 27	10 42	1 1	2 13	3 31	5 21	7 26	8 44
Acock's Green and South Yardley	arr.		9 31	10 46	1 5	2 16	3 35	5 25	7 30	8 47

Week Days.

		a.m.	a.m.	a.m.		a.m.	a.m.	N	a.m.	a.m.	a.m.	a.m.	a.m.	M	a.m.	a.m.		a.m.	a.m.
Acock's Green and South Yardley	dep.			6 20		7 15	7 38		7 50			8 19			8 42			
Tyseley	,,			6 23		7 19	7 25	7 41	7 53		8 17	8 22	8 34	8 37			8 47
Small Heath and Sparkbrook	,,	6 20	6 10	6 26		7 22	7 32	7 46	7 56		8 3	8 26	8 37	8 41		8 43	8 55
Bordesley	,,	6 25	6 14	6 30		7 26	7 36	7 49		8 0	9	8 31	8 41	8 46		8 51	8 53
Birmingham { Moor Street	arr.			6 33				7 30				8 37		8 44		
{ Snow Hill	,,	5 28	6 17			7 30		7 35		8 9	8 12	8 34		8 50		8 58

		a.m.	a.m.	a.m.	a.m.	a.m.	M	a.m.	a.m.	M	a.m.	p.m.	S	M	p.m.
Acock's Green and South Yardley	dep.	8 49				9 29			10 17		11 40			12 56	1 7
Tyseley	,,	8 52	9 0			9 32	9 34		10 21	11 14	11 44	12 2	12 10	1 0	1 11
Small Heath and Sparkbrook	,,	8 57		9 11	9 20	9 36	9 38		10 27	11 6	11 22	11 48	12 16	1 3	1 13
Bordesley	,,	9 2	9 4	9 11	9 20	9 40	9 42	10 1	10 31	11 12	11 52	12 19	12 17	1 5
Birmingham { Moor Street	arr.		9			9 45				11 25		12 12			1 20
{ Snow Hill	,,	9 5		9 15	9 26	9 45		10 5		10 35		11 55		

		MG	p.m.	p.m.		p.m.	G	MG		MS	p.m.	M		M	p.m.	p.m.		M
Acock's Green and South Yardley	dep.	1 38		1 59		2 9		2 20		2 42	2 49	3 19		3 42	4 44		5 20
Tyseley	,,	1 42	2 2	2 3		2 22	2 25		2 45	2 57	3 22		3 45	4 47		5 23	5 25
Small Heath and Sparkbrook	,,	1 46	2 7	2 7		2 15	2 26	2 35		2 49	3 2	3 51		3 49	3 56	4 54		5 27	5 31
Bordesley	,,	1 50	8	2 12		2 18	2 33		2 53	3 52		5 30
Birmingham { Moor Street	arr.		2 18					2 42		3 7	3 55		4 0	4 57		5 36
{ Snow Hill	,,	1 53		2 15							3 11			

		M		p.m.	p.m.		G	MG	M		M	G	M	p.m.	p.m.		M
Acock's Green and South Yardley	dep.	5 31				6 20	6 35		7 14			8 19	9 37		9 52		10 30
Tyseley	,,	5 36	5 56	6 2		6 10	6 43		7 20	7 26	7 54	8 22	8 41	9 24	9 57		10 35
Small Heath and Sparkbrook	,,	5 38	5 58	6 6		6 14	6 58	6 47	7 24	7 29	7 45	8 19	8 25	9 27	9 41		10 40
Bordesley	,,	5 42	6 2	6 10		6 19	6 52	6 51	7 28	7 33	8 30	8 50	9 31	9 46		10 44
Birmingham { Moor Street	arr.		6 5						7 35	7 55	8 25		9 34		
{ Snow Hill	,,	5 46		6 16		6 24	6 58	6 55	7 38			8 35	8 55	9 50		10 47

Sundays.

		a.m.	a.m.	a.m.	p.m.	p.m.	p.m.	p.m.	p.m.
Acock's Green and South Yardley	dep.	7 41	9 55	11 30	2 30	5 47	8 43	9 29	9 53
Tyseley	,,		9 59	11 33	2 38	5 50	8 47	9 32	9 57
Small Heath and Sparkbrook	,,	7 45	10 4	11 36	2 30	5 53	8 50	9 35	10 0
Bordesley	,,	7 50	10 8	11 41	2 41	5 53	8 55	9 40	10 5
Birmingham { Moor Street	arr.								
{ Snow Hill	,,	7 53	10 14	11 45	2 46	6 0	9 0	9 45	10 10

G—Saturdays excepted.
M—Rail Motor Car—one class only.
S—Saturdays only.
T—Thursdays and Saturdays only.

A Great Western Railway timetable for local services between Birmingham and Acocks Green.

Because of increasing demands on the station at Acocks Green, the GWR decided to provide a new building, and work commenced in 1906. This view shows the new station under construction, with the old station still in use on the right of the picture.

The new station at Acocks Green shortly after opening. This new facility appears to be very well used, with passengers waiting for trains.

A typical early twentieth-century local train, hauled by a GWR 0–4–2 Tank engine.

GWR 2–4–0 loco No. 1445 on a local train at Acocks Green in the first decade of the twentieth century.

A view of the new station at Acocks Green, looking towards Birmingham, in 1907.

A double-framed 4–4–0 hauls a London-bound express through Olton station. These engines were the mainstay of express motive power for London trains until replaced by Churchward's 'Saint' and 'Star' class 4–6–0s.

The very smart station at Solihull, serving a well-heeled town, at the turn of the century. Two local trains appear to be approaching the signal-box.

Another view of Solihull station, showing station buildings, footbridge, and signal-box.

Another 4–4–0 passes Widney Manor with a London train.

GWR 'Atbara' 4–4–0 No. 4147 *St Johns* passes Widney Manor and heads toward Knowle and Dorridge with an 'Up' express for Paddington.

Lapworth GWR.

The attractive main station building, complete with advertising hoardings, at Lapworth.

'Down' platform building at Lapworth. Also in view are the sidings and signal-box. The station sign informs passengers to change for Henley-in-Arden, the line to Henley running from here until the North Warwickshire Line opened in 1908.

Hatton junction, looking towards Birmingham. The station is a junction of the main London line and a branch, via Claverdon and Bearley, to Wilmcote and Stratford-upon-Avon. This branch was built by the GWR as part of its development of the shorter London route, built jointly with the Great Central Railway, in an effort to compete with the LNWR and its two-hour services between New Street and Euston. The branch was used to provide an express service from Paddington direct to Stratford which was becoming popular with American tourists, and the GWR provided a named train, the 'Shakespeare Express', for this service.

Another view of Hatton junction, showing the station building.

The station building at Bearley on the short branch to Wilmcote and Stratford-upon-Avon.

Bearley station, showing the station building, footbridge, and goods shed behind the platform.

Wilmcote old station building in derelict condition, with the signal-box beyond. The station was rebuilt when the North Warwickshire Line was opened, Wilmcote being situated on the new line.

The old station at Henley-in-Arden in the days when services to the town connected with the main London line at Hatton. Station staff pose by a local train of the period.

A new station was provided for Henley-in-Arden as part of the construction of the North Warwickshire Line, and the old one was abandoned, as can be seen here.

Just south of Danzey station on the North Warwickshire Line is an overbridge placed at an angle over a minor road, as can be seen in this 1958 view.

Earlswood station is situated in a rather attractive location. Passengers who wanted a day out at Earlswood Lakes, a local beauty spot popular with people from Birmingham, but were not familiar with the line would alight from trains here only to find that they were faced with a long walk to the lakes, whereas those in the know were aware that the next station on the line, the Lakes Halt, was right by the lakes.

BR 9F 2-10-0 No. 92215 passes Grimes Hill and Wythall station with a 'Down' freight. The station is still open but is now known just as Wythall. The wooden buildings have been demolished and replaced by bus shelter type structures. While the old station buildings were still standing, an iron stove would be used for heating in the winter months and cold passengers would be greeted by a cosy waiting room and a stove glowing a dull red. It was particularly welcome after a long walk to the station on cold and damp winter mornings for a train to work. The ticket collector, who was the only member of staff by the early 1970s, must have arrived very early in the morning to light up that stove, but passengers were very grateful to him. This station, along with the others on the North Warwickshire Line, has remained open thanks to the efforts of the Action Committee who have always been active in drawing attention to the benefits of the line and there is no doubt that the line remains very busy because of their efforts. It is still threatened with closure despite the number of passengers still using it but, I have no doubt, these threats will be actively resisted.

The railway bridge carrying the North Warwickshire Line over Baldwins Lane, between Yardley Wood and Shirley.

Yardley Wood station looking a little down at heel. The station platform was hit by a bomb during the Second World War, the blast demolishing six nearby shops.

Hall Green station, looking towards Stratford. The station building has now been demolished but the size of the structure suggests that the station was important, serving as it did a large suburb of Birmingham. During the summers of 1985 and 1986 the station was used as a starting point for steam excursions to Stratford, run by the Birmingham Railway Museum, and *Clun Castle* along with *Kohlapur* stopped here to pick up passengers.

Spring Road station, the last on the line, in the late 1970s. Joseph Lucas had a factory here, and the line passed under a bridge with the factory above on its way to Tyseley.

Back again at Tyseley junction, with a 'Hall' class 4–6–0 on a local train having just left the North Warwickshire Line, which curves away to the right in this view. On the left is the main line to Paddington which has been reduced to double track since the loss of London trains. Tyseley carriage sidings are on the extreme right.

SECTION FOUR

Industrial Railways

Birmingham had several industrial railways serving factories and linking with main lines in the city. Two of these, at Bournville and Longbridge, are shown here. Both connected with the Midland main line, but such systems have now virtually disappeared. Longbridge is unique in that it is still open and removes new motor cars from the Rover Group works. This, more than anything, shows that road transport is not the only answer and railways still have an important role to play in the transport infrastructure of Great Britain, despite the attempts of successive governments to destroy the British railway system.

Cadbury Ltd developed its own railway to supply raw materials to the works and remove finished chocolate products to its warehouse situated on the opposite side of the Birmingham and Worcester Canal. A link to the Midland Railway's West Suburban Line was also created to ease interchange between the two railways. Cadbury's built their own railway, as a connection between the two, to the standard gauge. Here, one of the company's locos heads a train up the bank to the connection with the Midland Railway in the early 1920s. The factory is in the background.

A late nineteenth-century view of Cadbury's railway line, close to the locoshed. The little 0–4–0 Saddle Tank engine was the first owned by the company. A siding was opened in 1884 when the factory was still small but, as it expanded, extensions were built until, by 1936, a complete railway, totalling six miles, encircled the whole manufacturing area.

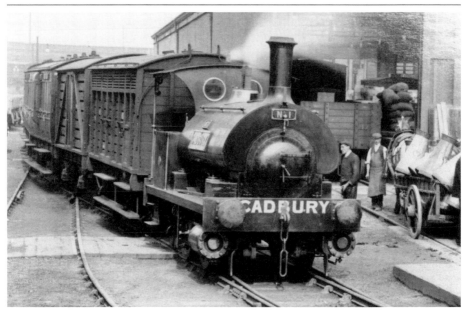

Cadbury's original No. 1 0–4–0 Saddle Tank loco runs vans past the warehouse. Also in view is a cart containing milk churns for use in the production of chocolate.

An advert for Cadbury's cocoa, one of the products carried on the company's railway.

Cadbury's No. 1 0–4–0 Side Tank loco, built by the Avonside Engine Company of Bristol in 1922 to replace the old Saddle Tank.

Another view of Cadbury's No. 1 outside the locoshed. This engine is now preserved and has been to several locations, starting out at the Dowty Preservation Society in Ashchurch until 1983. From there it went to Toddington until 1988, and is now at Tyseley, back in Birmingham.

Cadbury's locoshed in the 1950s, with a pair of the company's locos in view. No. 5 is blowing off steam at the cylinders, while an unidentified engine lies dormant in the shed. In an effort to maintain a clean environment at the works all steam engines were converted to coke firing in the early 1950s.

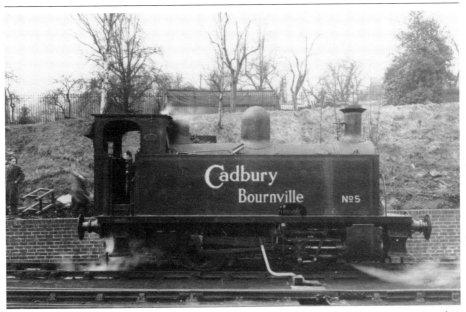

Cadbury's No. 5 loco, another Avonside-built product. Cadbury's engines were painted in deep red with gold lettering.

Cadbury's No. 6 0–4–0 Side Tank outside the locoshed. These locos had a 7 ft wheelbase.

A front view of Cadbury's No. 6 0–4–0 loco outside the shed.

Cadbury's No. 9 engine, built by Bagnall Ltd in 1950.

A front view of Cadbury's No. 9 in the mid-1950s.

Cadbury's No. 10 0–4–0 Saddle Tank, built by Peckett of Bristol in 1955. This engine was built to burn coke from new.

Employees at Cadbury's unload milk churns from a works train on to a horse-drawn cart. This view was probably taken just after the First World War, as the van from which the unloading was being done still bears the legend of the Midland Railway. After the Second World War more of the traffic to the factory was coming by road, and Cadbury's themselves were using road vans in increasing quantities from the mid-1950s. All of this threatened rail-borne freight and, by 1976, Cadbury's Railway had closed because the cost of keeping the railway running was becoming prohibitive.

Another company with its own internal railway was, and still is, the Austin Motor Company (now the Rover Group) at Longbridge, whose line linked with the Birmingham–Bristol main line via the Halesowen branch. One of the first locos used on the system was 0–6–0 Saddle Tank with the Welsh name of *Abernant*, built by Manning Wardle in 1921, and seen with her crew in 1924.

A 1906 advert for Austin cars. It is rather ironic that an industry that did so much damage to the railway system should use rail transport to move its products.

A section of the railway around the Longbridge car factory, with one of the company's 0–4–0 diesel engines, bought to replace steam traction in the 1960s. When the Halesowen branch was closed the former BR line and Longbridge station were bought by the company under an agreement dated 6 March 1968. The old station platform still exists but the

buildings were demolished. The old signal-box still belongs to BR and is operated by BR staff; the Rover Group pays for upkeep and the signalman's wages. The section of line between the Bristol main line and the old Longbridge station is still BR owned and joins the main line just beyond the new Longbridge station.

Little 0–6–0 Saddle Tank *Emily*, built by Manning Wardle in 1901, rests at the buffer stops behind the factory.

A nice picture of *Emily* inside the locoshed, showing footplate details. The engine is being serviced by Austin employees.

Kitson built *Austin 1* 0–6–0 Saddle Tank on the works railway. The loco was built in 1932.

The engine driver cleans the tank of *Austin 3* 0–6–0 Saddle Tank, built by the Hunslet Engine Company in 1937.

A broadside view of *Austin 3*, showing the company's crest on the cabside.

A rather grubby looking *Austin 11* 0–6–0 Saddle Tank, built by Hunslet in 1936.

Ex-War Department No. 1938, an American-built engine brought into the UK for the war effort, was purchased by Austin in July 1947 and named *Ada*. The engine was ideal for the heavy freight traffic demanded of it.

Large 0–6–0 Saddle Tank *Vulcan*, built by Bagnall in 1950 and used on the railway until replaced by diesel locos.

Sister engine *Victor* (should it be 'brother' in this case?), also built by Bagnall in 1951. Both of these engines have now been preserved, one making a brief appearance on the Llangollen Railway.

An atmospheric night-time picture of the Longbridge works and railway, with a rake of 'Cartic' car-carrying railway vehicles waiting for loading with newly produced cars. The railway is still very much in use and likely to be so for the forseeable future.

Acknowledgements

I should like to record my thanks to all who have helped with photographs used in this project, including Jim Roberts, Roger Carpenter, R.M. Casserley, and Frank Jones.

Special thanks to Helen Davies of the library at Cadbury Ltd for her unending patience in dealing with my many enquiries; David Ibbotson, who supplied many photographs used in this book and also gave much background information; and Trevor Cousens who provided pictures of the Longbridge railway, and to the Rover Group for allowing their use.